WHISPERS TO EMBERS

THE RED INK GUILD'S VERSION

SMRIBELLA YAGNYATHRI

BookLeaf Publishing

India | USA | UK

Copyright © SMRIBELLA YAGNYATHRI
All Rights Reserved.

This book has been self-published with all reasonable efforts taken to make the material error-free by the author. No part of this book shall be used, reproduced in any manner whatsoever without written permission from the author, except in the case of brief quotations embodied in critical articles and reviews.

The Author of this book is solely responsible and liable for its content including but not limited to the views, representations, descriptions, statements, information, opinions, and references ["Content"]. The Content of this book shall not constitute or be construed or deemed to reflect the opinion or expression of the Publisher or Editor. Neither the Publisher nor Editor endorse or approve the Content of this book or guarantee the reliability, accuracy, or completeness of the Content published herein and do not make any representations or warranties of any kind, express or implied, including but not limited to the implied warranties of merchantability, fitness for a particular purpose.

The Publisher and Editor shall not be liable whatsoever...

Made with ❤ on the BookLeaf Publishing Platform
www.bookleafpub.in
www.bookleafpub.com

Dedication

"To the years of restless nights
that sparked my heart,
To the truths, often addressed to
the fire,
May these verses speak the
whispers we once feared to utter."

Preface

Each poem is a collection of broken verses, sparked by raw emotions and quiet vulnerability. Penned in the stillness of sleepless nights, they began as letters addressed to the fire.

Caught in the chaos of coming of age, I dared to ink my truth, hoping my silent screams might lend a voice to those burdened by the weight of unspoken words. These pages are haunted by the ghosts I long to bury and the phoenix that rose from their ashes.

Today, I remain a flicker of that flame, molded by the goddess of time. Echoing the restless thoughts of a girl aging from 16 to 22—fleeting phases of my life now made permanent in words.

Dear reader, within these verses lies a journey through heartache, quiet rebellion, healing, and acceptance. From adolescence to adulthood, from questioning society to embracing history and culture, and finally, to the bonds of friendship and love that both break and build us—these are stories of struggle, defiance, passion, and resilience.

Perhaps, in these words, you will find a friend who shares both the warmth and the burn of truths that are personal yet universal.

To the relentless escapists: may these verses awaken the lost poet in you,

stirring the courage to voice the truths
you have been too shy or afraid to speak
aloud.

— **FROM THE Red Ink Guild**

Acknowledgements

This book was once a mere fragment of my imagination. I owe immense gratitude to the **restless moments** and the relentless people who awakened the poet within me.

A special thanks to my friends–
A, for introducing me to the beauty of poetry;
TM and **JD**, whose patient ears nurtured my thoughts and writing;
AP, for motivating me to act on my dreams; and
B, for breathing life into a part of me I once believed to be nonexistent.

To my **mother**, **brother**, **grandmother**, **father**, and **uncle**—your roles in my life and poems are beyond the reach of words.

My heartfelt appreciation to **T.S.**, whose inquisitive songwriting inspired me to explore the art of channeling raw emotions into verses.

A shoutout to those **unnamed** yet unforgettable—your presence has left an imprint on my journey and these pages.

And most importantly, to you, **dear reader**, for becoming the keepers of these whispers. Without you, these poems would remain mere echoes in the quiet.

Thank you!

Index

Phase I:
Childhood, Change, Challenges and Coming of Age

1. "Letters to the Moon"

If I got swept up in the tides of time,
Dragged down to when life lost its shine,
I would hug the little version of mine,
"One day everything will be fine."

I remember writing letters to my future self,
Speaking to the moon, hoping its light would guide me to myself,

*Wishing that she lived our
dreams soon enough,
And meet her past self.*

*I can't help but wonder,
Would she be proud of herself,
Or wish I had done more for
myself?
Cling to her papers, reveal our
souls in her poems,
Waiting for us to meet once
again.*

*I would tell her to stick to her
guns,*

Because often life is not as fun,
"But know that soon there will be
sun,"
Even when she feels there's none.

Can't resist but think of this,
Would she have faith in me?
Or hope some other version to
be?
Believe in the idea of we,
Work towards a future she can't
yet see.

Cling to her brushes and paints,
And express us in those colors,

Tell her that life's a canvas,
sometimes just let it taint,
To learn and grow, we aren't
meant to be saints.
No reason to worry or faint.

Because I know I'd love for her to
age,
Burning bridges and turning each
page.
Don't let it slip through the
haze,
Each chapter is only just a
phase.
Life is just like a maze,

Walk, run, and fall,
You will be amazed.

2. "The Pursuit of Innocence"

Smiling among the vibrant balloons,
She was the joy, the life of the room.
Who would warn of childhood slipping away soon,
Taking with it all that she loved under the moon?

When happiness was found in every little thing,

Now she feared what life would bring.
Once she'd sleep without a care,
Dreams as sweet as the songs her mother would share.

Now, peaceful sleep seems but a dare,
Haunted by nightmares lingering in the air.
Silent screams and tears that would sting,
Life a burden, with no one to cling.

Yet still, she was as innocent and bold,
As the child inside her, who never wished to grow old.
Patiently braving the bitter cold,
With a heart of steel, though her spirit was gold.

Countless battles she fought,
Thanks to the lessons her mother taught—
In this abyss, her one true wealth:
A foundation stronger than any earthly stealth.

Dancing to society's tunes was
never her thought,
She followed the rhythm only
her inner child caught.
To prove to herself, she was
worth the cost,
To realize she's a typhoon, and
all was not lost.

3. "Rooted and Rising"

Born into love and blissful grace,
A pampered princess, she was raised.
If only she'd known it was a phase,
Her mother's passing left her dazed.
Memories faded, and erased,
As a defense mechanism, her heart embraced.

A fate so bittersweet made life a dead end,
In her mother's farewell, she lost her best friend.
But a blessing in disguise did send,
In her brother's first cry, she found a love to defend.
Slowly but surely, her heart began to mend,
Yet often, she felt she played pretend,
As life continued, in joy and sorrow's blend.

Dusk to dawn, fortnights to fourteen years,

In her grandmother's care, she cast aside her tears.

In her father's presence, she ran to the frontiers.

With every step, she let go of her doubts and fought her fears.

Adolescence then gifted her loyal friends and honest peers.

She aced her school and silenced fools, fueled by their cheers.

Life now seemed too good to be true,

For roses have thorns too, in her
heart she knew.
Lingering feelings in shades of
blue,
Dreading the calm before the
storm, she grew.
As lessons were learned from
Nancy Drew,
Her perceptive eyes missed not a
clue.

Then, her father's choice
provoked feelings so strong,
With wounds old and new, life
seemed hard and long.

She hid herself in her paintings
and songs,
As her faith and friends pushed
her on.
The road once taken that
appeared so wrong,
Led her to a loving home, where
she now belongs.

What's in her future? Time can't
yet say.
But she's sure she'll make her
own way.
As the guiding lights bright as
day,

Her love and friends won't let her stray.

Weathering winter storms, she's learned to sway.

Now she knows she's here to stay.

4. "Beautiful Scars"

Staring at the moonlit beams in the sky,
She found solace beneath the veil of night.
Painting her emotions, her thoughts soaring high,
Even in the darkest hour, she remained a beautiful sight.

Falling like dominoes, her black strands of hair,
Framed her face, lost in sorrows deep.

*Surfacing memories too painful
to bear,*
*Her slender fingers traced secrets
she'd keep.*

*Her skin, adorned with stories of
battles fought,*
*To the world, they seemed like
nasty marks.*
*But to her, they were beautiful
scars,*
*Souvenirs of strength of her life's
arc.*

*Her glimmer of hope was the
stars shining bright,
Searching for meaning, refusing
to cry.
Her hazel-brown eyes charted
the constellations' light,
As a shooting star answered her
questions of why.
In the stillness of the night, life
finally felt right.*

Phase II:
Society, Expectations, Resistance, Call to Action.

5. "Patriarchal Privilege"

Invisible threads of age-old weight,

Forget, she once was worshipped,

in a culture great,

As they weave around society's state.

What some call a worthless debate,

Are the same who decide our fate.

Few voices whisper, trying to relate,

Yet their efforts fall short—too little, too late.

In a supposed world of order and law,
A silent privilege ignores its major flaw.
Often, her destiny she strives to draw,
Yet her independence yearns to thaw.
For equality and freedom, her fingers still claw—
Always a "she" with the short end of the straw.

In urban cities and boardroom
meets,
Though her confidence peaks,
She's expected to balance work
and home with ease,
While they walk around,
unbothered in the streets.
She's catcalled and stared at as
they tease.
Empowerment now feels like a
deceit—
Unequal pay to their egos
appease.

Generations of silent oppression,
In rural villages, overlooked suppression,
Ostracism pushing her into depression.
God forbid her right to speech and expression.
"How dare she question such possession?"
Shunning young voices of truth, their new obsession—
"Woke feminists" dismissed with aggression.

A daughter, a sister, a wife, a mother,
Her many names,
Yet over her own life, few claims.
Always a pawn in misogynistic games,
Forever the subject of unjust blames.
She's had enough of her diminishing flames.
Her destiny is hers to reclaim.

6. "Chained Dreams"

Whispers down the street of the devil they claim I must be;
Another blow to my fragile sanity,
Simply because I didn't fit their fantasy
Or follow the rules they set for you and me.

This world never offered us a fair treat.
Girls who dream are left to stand on their feet,

Bound by the chains of reality,
But now, let's challenge this so-
called normalcy,
So that girls like us don't have to
run and flee.

Silent pleas, cries of defeat,
Echo through generations, past
and complete.
Oh world, where is your
morality?
Oh girls, let's rise above this
fallacy!
It's time to be free.

7. "Wings of Rebirth"

Breathless and panting, as she stood,

She decided to disappear for good.

She ran as fast as she could,

For she had never been understood.

She ran, summoning every ounce of might,

Into the enchanted forest, through woods of night.

Her weary feet carried her far,

To a realm untouched, guided by
a burning star.

The faint flicker of hope burned
deep within,
A quiet flame, igniting the
journey to begin.
Burning brighter with every step,
igniting her wandering heart,
A glimmer of light refusing to
depart.

Through every sacrifice, every
ache endured,

She moved forward; her resolve assured.
With every step, the pain lingered,
Yet her heart, resolute, to the forest it whispered.

A faint, soft glow encircled her,
As eagle eyes, keen and sharp, began to stir.
Gazing into the void, she patiently waited,
For the fallen warrior, long forsaken, to be reinstated.

For the golden rays of the lost to
arise,
Reincarnating beneath the open
skies,
Bringing light to what was
before, never to die.
She yearned to spread her wings
high.

And when the time comes, she
will dive,
Into clear waters, reborn and
alive.

8. "An Angles Awakening"

Engulfed in the chaos of emotion,
Caged in the prison of her own demons,
She was no damsel in distress,
But an angel fallen in the depths of hopeless oceans.

Patiently waiting for the passing of seasons,
Her frail soul, weary, lay to rest,
Pining for a long-lost reflection.

And then, a fleeting wave of devotion
Crashed upon her shore with streams of reason,
Igniting the spark of resurrection.

Her yearning heart, now full of passion,
And a sense of newfound vision.
Her single-minded obsession:
To flee the false paradise of Eden.

Phase III:
History, Culture, Belief, and Reckoning.

9. "Daughter of the Earth"

As sweet scents of spring in nature bloom,
A heavenly blessing began to loom.
For a kingdom then shed its shrouds of gloom.
The princess rose from the earth's womb,
As elegant and radiant as the moon.

The winds whispered tales of the beauty wise,

To cities far under distant skies.
Kindness and grace beheld in her lotus eyes,
Silent strength in innocent disguise
Heaved the mighty bow to everyone's surprise.

As the maiden grew in the embrace of time,
Several royals sought her in a challenge fine.
But only one strung fate's grand design—

*Two hearts entwined in marriage
divine.*
*Her loyalty and devotion,
eternally aligned.*

*The wheels of fortune weaved
out of turn,*
*Flickers of doubt, shadows in the
palace churned.*
*Exiled to the forest, to fulfill a
father's concern,*
*Yet her resolve forged and
burned,*
*As a kingdom left behind awaited
their return.*

In the sacred groves, she felt at home,
Unbeknownst to her, as dangers roamed.
With seeds of desire and revenge sown,
A demon disguised as a sage was shown.
But to her lord, she stayed sworn.

Though captive, in devil's deceit,
she wasn't bound.

Despite the tricks and threats,
she stood her ground.
Weeping tears, she longed to be
found,
As she waited, her prince then
came around.
A queen, she was soon to be
crowned?

But her destiny, she was yet to
understand.
Through trials dark, fire sparks
took her stand,
Yet failed to hush the
reprimand.

Tendrils of fate again twisted her hand,
Banished alone, out of her own land.

She raised her sons with love and grace.
Swallowed by the soil without a trace,
She returned to her mother's embrace.
Her legacy, a legend none can erase,
A goddess worshipped across time and space.

10. "Forged in Fire"

On a dawn, both mystic and auspicious,

Crystal-clear skies embraced the sun's caress,

Sweet incense swept through the wind so propitious,

As saints gathered 'round a sacred pyre,

Chants and hymns stirred by a king's desire—

A son to avenge the sire.

As if the heavens grew
capricious,
Dark clouds gathered, summoned
by a sorceress,
Engulfed in acrid smoke, fierce
and ferocious,
Rose the princess, born of fire.
A daughter, nurtured by her
father's vengeful desire,
Destined to stir a dynasty's
smother.

On the horizon graced another
morrow auspicious,

*As royals far and wide gathered
for ceremony propitious,
Seeking the princess's hand in a
challenge quite ambitious.
Many arrows flew, their marks
amiss,
Only one pierced through, an
archer in disguise,
Igniting a spark, a wish for
marital bliss.*

*As if the heavens turned
vicious,
A mother's command, so pious.*

The maiden became a wife, to not one, but five.

Gifted a barren forest, forsaken and forlorn,
From ashes to riches, a new kingdom was born.
And she rose as an empress, her legacy adorned.

11. "The Legacy of Flames"

Seasons passed, as time molded the empress.

Yet she enjoyed no riches, but suffered a fate so malicious.

The place of illusions brought forth her distress,

Dragged through courts of the pompous and pretentious.

A slave, a pawn in the games of dice,

The dark maiden prayed, a tear-soaked face.

*Her lotus-eyed friend, the blue
one, was her saving grace.*

*Cursed to exile, a queen in
disguise,*
*Suffering humiliations, the
maiden grew wise.*

*The 14th year dawned, and war
shattered the skies.*
*The burning wood and ash saw a
goddess rise.*
*Her long strands adorned with a
crown, the blood of her woes,*

*Turning wrongs to rights, she
reclaimed her vows.*

*Yet the gods, still blind to her
pain and plight,*
*Her children consumed by the
reign of night.*

*Yet she rose, like fire undwindled
—*

*A queen, a warrior, a spirit
rekindled.*
*Her pain and wrath, from battles
fought, now lessons sublime.*

Her legacy forever etched in history and time.

12. "Serenades of Shyam"

Tender fingers play the flute, singing melodies, swaying the soul.

Lotus eyes, shining bright, pierce through my heart, and the universe whole.

His mysterious smile lights up the face, radiant as the moon 'midst dark monsoon clouds.

Peacock feathers crown his dark curls, an eternal escape from entangling shrouds.

From the cosmic ocean's depths,
where creation's waves swell,
In the Serpent King's embrace,
the Infinite One and the Mother
Goddess dwell.
From his serene slumber, the
dance of destruction looms,
As celestial consciousness, time
and space, from the lotus
blooms.

With reincarnations on earth, in
each divine birth, a purpose he
serves,

As the fish saves scriptures, the
tortoise churns immortal nectar,
the boar rescues earth—life he
preserves.
The savior then rose in the lion's
protective roar, the dwarf's
humble strides, and the axe's
might.
Then the prince's arrows and
words set the world right.

The cowherd, all-knowing,
guides his flock across fields of
illusion,

As the charioteer steers the lost
warrior towards duty, despite
confusion.
In the words of calm wisdom, the
eternal truth resounds,
Awaiting his return in forms
anew, the cyclic end now bound.

As the soil tells his tales and the
wind whispers his name,
Within each being rests his
undying flame.
As the pages of history and the
future's mystery seek his trace,

*With every breath, my soul
craves for his grace.*

*In humble reverence to him, I
bow and surrender,*
*For in his love, trials and
triumphs all endure.*
*Through silent prayers, as he
nurtures and forgives,*
*In his devotion, I hope my spirit
forevermore lives.*

13. "Guardians of Swarajya"

From snow-clad peaks kissing the sky,
Across forests lush and deserts desolate,
To sacred rivers swallowed by oceans wide,
Stretched an ancient culture, of warriors pious and great.

Majestic temples hum tales of gods who walked past,
Forgotten forts of empires with sacrifices tall,

A golden bird soared, as noble
kings ruled steadfast.
Their legacy etched in the pages
of history's thrall.

The golden ages faded into
medieval nights,
Eying the wealth, as invaders
broke the walls.
A shield of unyielding spirits
gave their lives,
Echoes of courageous war cries
defending the mother's fall.

Amidst colonial chains, the fire of freedom burned,
Revolutionary souls inspired with blood, sweat, and tears.
From the ashes of legends past, resistance returned.
A new era dawned as wounds conquered fears.

In uniformed ranks, sons and daughters of the soil on frontiers stand,
Under the banners of historic valiance, brave hearts march on.

Eliminating every threat and treachery against this land,
From devotions depth's to power's heights, the unsung legacy lives on.

14. "A Mother's Wrath"

I know there's much at stake,
Yet we will live to tell the tale.
In the dead of night, for the human race,
Dangers lurk, leaving trails.

Showers of peace and quiet for earthlings to take,
The world once free, now left in disgrace.
Stabbed by mankind, a deceitful snake,
Testing and taunting fate.

Once the loving force that gave
life's grace,
Mother Nature has her mighty
ways.
Reminds her guests of their
rightful place,
For she is no man's slave.

In sorrow's embrace, her wrath
we face.
For survival of the fittest, we
must brace.
Kneel, for mercy we must seek;

*Pray for humanity, humble and
meek.*

*Thy mother, grant forgiveness to
the human race,*
If our hearts can still reach,
*To learn again the lessons she's
bound to preach.*

Phase IV:
Friendships, Loss, Longing and Love!

15. "Ride or Die"

The first hello in 3rd standard,
junior college, and webcam
chats,
Turned to discussions post-
school, tuitions, and online
class.
We stuck through despite the
distance and spats,
And I found a friend in him and
her.

For projects and end terms, with
her I conferred.

She skipped lectures just to wipe
my tears.
From morning walks to late-
night talks,
The lines then blurred—
A safe space to let out my fears.

From inside jokes to life advice,
She's my partner in crime.
Takes my stand, corrects my
flaws, still defends my vice.
Our beautiful bond transcends
time.
For she's my soul sister.

*When the rollercoaster of life led
me into an abyss,*
He was present through all of it.
*His friendship brought me some
solace;*
He made sure I never quit.
*In the dark days, he seemed a
vesper.*

*The calm to my chaos and vice
versa.*
*He reads me like a well-known
chapter—*
*Sometimes out of sync, but no
need to reverse.*

We are yet to see what comes
after,
He's always there, an active
listener.

Hope our silly fights give way to
endless laughs,
Because through thick and thin,
they stuck by.
I'll be there to guide them across
treacherous paths.
They'll forever be my ride or
die,
For they're the best friends my
heart holds dear.

16. "Wish I Wrote You a Love Song!"

You don't know the nights I cried all alone,
Wondering why you left me on my own,
Sprawled on the cold, hard floor.
How could you just walk out the door?
Our so-called friends left me there to die,
Staring up at the black, empty sky.

I want to say I hate you, if only it were true,

But I won't waste my breath, no, not on you.

No other choice—so I'm through.

The ghosts of your past, they haunt my mind,

I feel like prey, hunted and confined.

I know now that your exes didn't lie.

I want to write you a hate song, why deny?

A song that shames you for all you've done,

But who'd believe me? No, not anyone.
If I said you gave me a death I didn't deserve,
For a crime you committed, you have some nerve.

I am just a girl who dreamed,
But you burned them to the ground as I screamed.
I want to say I hate you,
But I won't waste my breath on you.
You are the "Superstar," calling me names,

It's time to end your stupid little games.

Stabbing me in the same old wounds,

Making the world dance to your tunes.

But it's okay, there will be new moons,

And you'll soon cry to my croons.

I want to write you a hate song.

Well, I'm sorry if my hurt's your knife.

Now you're just another chapter
in my life.
One day, you'll be a song I
wrote,
In the pages of a book, a
forgotten quote.
Just another song in a concert,
A pointless topic to divert.

Soon you'll have nowhere to hide
and run.
I want to say I hate you, but why
lie?
Maybe deep down, I hoped you
were the one.

I wish I could love you; let's not be shy!

17. "The Touch of Twilight."

In the fading cascades of the
day,
Stood a silhouette still by the
bay.
Shadows whispered in shades of
grey,
Engulfing the soul who lost its
way.

As the sky bled in hues of
crimson and gold,
Flashes of secret promises quietly
unfold.

Once waves of warmth, now
chilling and cold,
The sand met the sea where tales
remain untold.

For now, thoughts of old mere
whispers in the breeze,
And ghosts of laughter faint in
the rustling trees.
Forgotten forever in the depths
of the seas,
How one wished that time would
forever freeze.

Effortless thoughts of a life once made,
Memories of its death yet to fade.
Skin and bones, worn and frayed,
Praying for the cruel fate to be swayed.

As twilight kissed the edge of the shore,
The soul wondered, would dusk meet dawn once more?
Or a fathom of unsung folklore,
Fade into silence forevermore.

18. "Beyond the Distance"

Our house of dreams was built on trust,
With careful designs in every part,
Now haunted by echoes of silent screams,
Ghosted by us.

Cobwebs rest on our beloved art,
Iron gates, once strong, now coated in rust.

*Where ivy bloomed, rose thorns
creep into my heart.*

*Sparkling silver fades to dust,
Shining bright within our walls
at the start.
This road to home seems long,
lost and unjust,
Swallowed by a maze too tall,
Built to keep us apart.*

*Our spirit aches, bruised black
and blue,
Hearts once red now burn
scarlet, maroon.*

How did we end up here, without
a single clue?
The pictures of the life we drew
Now fade, dissolving far too
soon.

In our garden, where sweet
scents are meant to bloom,
A whirlwind whispers omens of
doom.
In warm sunlight, our promises
were true—
Maybe we lived inside a fragile
cocoon.

I feel our heartlines going flat,
But my feet retrace the grass to
our spot.
I think we are worth more than
that—
More than our efforts that fell
short.

The clear waters where we once
sat
Reflect a love we nearly lost.
But now, I see where we are at.

Our forlorn hearts still seek their
north,

*The boat sails beyond all
combat.
I know we have been through a
lot,
Tangled in stubborn knots—
This long distance is worth the
shot.*

19. "Feminine Urges"

Whispers trace the edges of the mind,
Where passion seeks permission to unwind.
The teasing touch, firm yet kind,
Sparks a desire, burning and blind.
As fevered dreams of souls aligned,
The rhythm of two hearts now combined.

A silent storm brews beneath the skies,
Where whispers of vows forge strong ties.
Meeting of skin and trembling thighs,
Leads closer and closer to unworldly highs.
In a warm embrace where surrender soon lies,
A loving caress forsakes the need for disguise.

A holy gospel, a ghost of a breath,

As gentle fingers trace secret depths.
In cravings as addictive as meth,
Lie the gasps of tiny euphoric death.
The price of innocence' theft,
Prying at intense feelings,
fleeting rest.

20. "Pillow Talk"

Passionate prayers, whispered words,
Under night's blanket, moments spurred.

In his warmth, I felt a golden rush,
As he confessed, I was still his crush.
"Was he mine?" it hung heavy in the hush,
My heart leaped, full and lush.

His question answered with my
rosy blush,
My face alight and flush.

Then his mask betrayed a subtle
smile,
And my heart felt free, no longer
in exile.

As we enjoyed our peaceful
bliss,
I came alive as if sun-kissed.
"He liked his name on my red
lips,"

His touch, a promise I couldn't resist.
My heart, once astray and amiss,
In his arms, my doubts all dismissed.

In the dark, as feelings stirred,
In acts of love, I felt heard.

Hazel brown eyes stared deep into mine,
In their depths, I found a love divine.

"Don't let go of that sparkle and
shine,
I wish you knew you're more
than just fine."
And in his words, I felt at my
prime,
Grateful that we crossed the
line.

His soothing words fought my
darkest fears,
A bandage to years of tears.

In his embrace, felt as if all was
won.

As his waves crashed my shore, I came undone.
Life was meant to be fun.
And in that moment, I hoped he was the one,
For in his love, I was forever spun.
Better for me, there would be none.

In his heart was my true home,
An unconditional love, where I'd never feel alone.

21. "All's well that ends well!"

Prayers whispered for a divine intervention,
As hearts once craved for timeless affection.
The goddess of timing beheld pure intention,
Showering her blessings through a cosmic connection.
For two lost souls, guided by her direction,
Found fathoms of themselves in each other's reflection.

In a beautiful symphony, when all starts align,

Two lives intertwine once parallel lines.

As devils of longing and separation now resign,

Past heartbreaks seem like destiny's designs.

As fire and air now appear like a twin sign,

Love, once out of reach, blooms and shines.

As showers turned to winter storms,
Their love stood strong, breaking the norms.
For true love endures and seldom fails,
As the goddess tests, their faith prevails.
Through trials of fate, their bond transforms,
And by love's grace, their spirit again warms.

So, all's well that ends well,

As in hopeless romance, two spirits fell.

Souls forever bound in Cupid's spell,

As their love story a heart yearns to tell again.

A calm escape where chaos may dwell,

In each embrace, all fears die and quell.

www.ingramcontent.com/pod-product-compliance
Lightning Source LLC
Chambersburg PA
CBHW070543160726
48003CB00005B/1855